SWEDEN

DENMARK

BRUNSWICK
BRANDENBURG

Germany

Wittenberg

HESSE
SAXONY

AINZ

HOLY
ROMAN EMPIRE

POLAND

Cracow

WITZERLAND

MILAN
Pavia
Lodi
Parma
Terraferma
Vicenza
Padua
MANTUA
FERRARA
Bologna
Forlì
Rimini
GENOA
VENICE

O T T O M A N

CONSTANTINOPLE

FLORENCE
River Arno
Urbino
SIENA
PAPAL
STATES

River Tiber
ROME

Italy

NAPLES

E M P I R E

Greece

EAN SEA

N
W   E
S

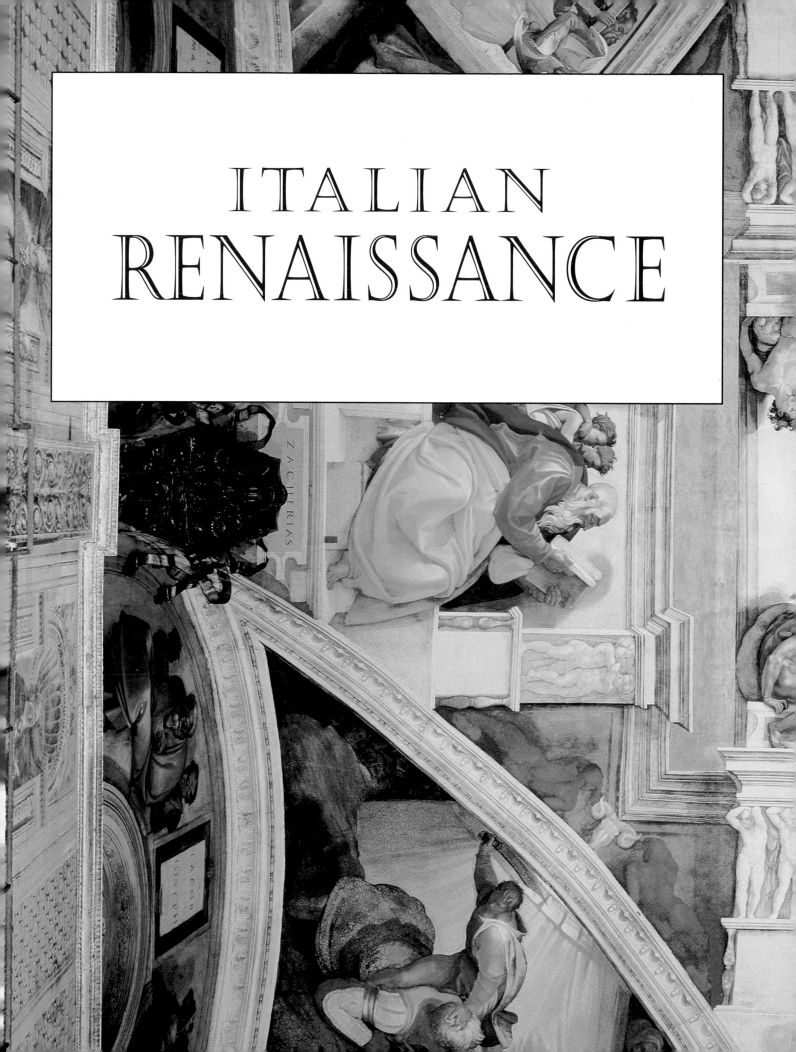

ITALIAN
RENAISSANCE

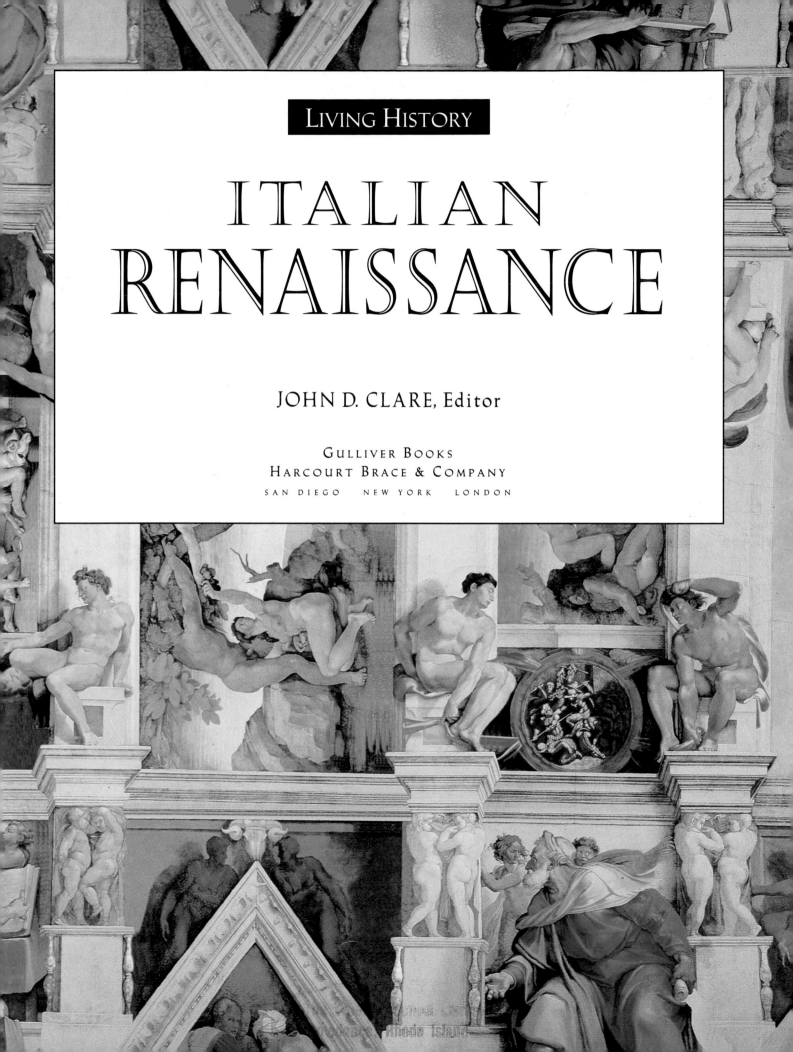

LIVING HISTORY

ITALIAN RENAISSANCE

JOHN D. CLARE, Editor

GULLIVER BOOKS
HARCOURT BRACE & COMPANY
SAN DIEGO   NEW YORK   LONDON

HARCOURT
BRACE

First published in Great Britain in 1994 by Riverswift, Random House

First U.S. edition 1995

Library of Congress Cataloging-in-Publication Data
Italian Renaissance/John D. Clare, editor.
p.   cm. — (Living history)
"Gulliver Books."
Includes index.
ISBN 0-15-200088-7
1. Italy — Civilization — 1268–1559 — Juvenile literature.
2. Renaissance — Italy — Juvenile literature. [1. Italy —
Civilization — 1268–1559. 2. Renaissance — Italy.] I. Clare, John
D., 1952–   . II. Series: Living history (San Diego, Calif.)
DG445.I77 1995
945'.05 — dc20   94-26637

Director of Photography   Tymn Lintell
Photography   Charles Best
Art Director   Dalia Hartman
Production Manager, Photography   Fiona Nicholson
Typesetting   Thompson Type, San Diego, California
Reproduction   HBM Print Pte Ltd, Singapore

ACKNOWLEDGMENTS

Historical Advisor: Dr. Alan Millen, University of Kent. **Historical Consultant:** Richard Mackenney. **Casting:** Piccolo Teatro, Siena; Teatro Comunale di Firenze. **Fresco Consultant:** Faith Vincent. **Jacket Concept:** Peter Bennett. **Location Consultants:** Alta Macadam and Sammie Daniels. **Location Finders:** William Larson and Antony Parks. **Map and Timeline:** John Laing. **Map Illustrations:** David Wire. **Photography Assistant:** Michael Harvey. **Transport:** Peter Knight, Road Runner Film Services.

Additional photographs: Ancient Art and Architecture Collection: p. 17 top; p. 24 bottom. Ashmolean Museum, Oxford: pp. 36–37. Biblioteca Medicea Laurenziana, Florence: p. 46 bottom. Bibliothèque de l'Institut de France, Paris: p. 41 middle left. Bridgeman Art Library, London: Christie's London pp. 54–55; Museo Real Academia de Bellas Artes, Madrid pp. 58–59; British Library p. 63 bottom right. British Library: p. 62 bottom right. A. F. Kirsting: p. 10 top. National Gallery, London: (detail) pp. 32–33; (detail) p. 40 top right. Nippon Television Network Corporation, Tokyo 1991: (details) pp. 1–5. Antony Parks: front cover, background landscape; pp. 44–45. Royal Collection: p. 23 top right; p. 38 middle left. Scala, Florence: p. 6; p. 7 (2); p. 9 (2); (detail) pp. 12–13; p. 13 top; p. 14 bottom right; pp. 18–19 (4); (detail of head by Fra Angelico) p. 21; p. 22; p. 23 bottom; p. 26 middle left; (detail) pp. 26–27; p. 27 bottom right; p. 31 top; p. 33 top; (detail) pp. 40–41; p. 44 (2); p. 45; p. 48 top; (detail) pp. 48–49; (detail) pp. 52–53; p. 62 top. The Wellcome Institute Library, London: p. 60.

Contents

A Time of Change

In 1400, northern Italy was among the richest areas of Europe. The Holy Roman Emperor, whose title was created when the Catholic Church attempted to restore the Roman Empire in western Europe, was the nominal overlord of this part of Italy as well as Germany. In fact, though, the lands of the Holy Roman Empire were filled with small states, many of which resisted or were independent of the emperor's authority.

The prosperous republics of Florence and Venice were among the most important states in Italy. Florence was a great cloth-making and banking center. Venice controlled a small empire in the Mediterranean. In these two cities as well as in Rome, which was ruled by the pope, and a handful of other Italian states, art and learning began to flourish in the 15th century.

No major war or political change separated the early 15th century from earlier times, but people living in Italy nonetheless began to have the sense that they were liv-

ing in a "new age." The people who first championed this new age were known as humanists. The humanists held that civili-

zation had reached its height in ancient Greece and Rome. Their own time, they claimed, was defined by a rebirth (or a "renaissance") of learning that promised to revive the "ancient elegance" that somehow had been lost. During the 15th and 16th centuries, the humanists consciously tried to change the whole of society — politics, the arts and literature, learning, manners, and religion — to imitate and perhaps surpass what they saw as the glories of the ancient cultures of Greece and Rome.

LEAVING BEHIND THE MIDDLE AGES

The term Middle Ages was first used by the Italian humanist Flavio Biondo (1392–1463) to describe the years between the fall of Rome and his own times. To Renaissance humanists, antiquity seemed to have a "pure, pristine radiance," and the Middle Ages represented a dark period of stagnation when many of the achievements of classical culture had been forgotten.

Humanist writers criticized scholars who followed the traditions of the Middle Ages as out-of-date and even barbarous. In contrast, they tried to learn as much as they could about classical times and described themselves as "universal men" with a broad knowledge of all subjects. To emphasize the difference in their outlook, many humanists abandoned the medieval Gothic script and adopted an italic style of handwriting, which they mistakenly thought was used in classical times.

In addition to seeking greater knowledge of the classical world, the artists and thinkers of the Renaissance also tried to discover more about the physical world around them. By studying the appearance of buildings, the architect Filippo Brunelleschi (1377–1466), for example, developed a system of mathematical perspective to help painters represent three-dimensional scenes on a flat surface. The artist Leonardo da Vinci (1452–1519) dissected human corpses to learn more about anatomy. Mapmakers, including Paolo Toscanelli (1397–1482), rejected medieval traditions of mapmaking, which were based on symbolism, and instead attempted to represent the world to scale, filling out their maps with the latest geographical discoveries. Great parts of the world were still unknown to Europeans, but the maps created by Toscanelli and other Renaissance mapmakers

were of much more help to explorers than earlier medieval maps would have been.

THE START OF THE MODERN WORLD?

Looking back, many writers of the late 19th century saw the Renaissance as the beginning of the modern age. The English historian J. A. Symonds described the Renaissance as the time when "humanity awoke as it were from slumber and began to live." According to Symonds, medieval people were "semi-barbarous . . . pathetic . . . [living] amidst stupidity and ignorance . . . devoted by superstition to saints and by sorcery to the devil." No wonder he decided that the Renaissance was "the liberation of humanity from a dungeon."

Nowadays historians are more ready to accept that the Middle Ages had scholars, artists, and architects of genius. Some have even suggested that the years from 1400 to 1600, the years of the Renaissance, were "the flowering of the Middle Ages." But whether the Renaissance represented the culmination of the Middle Ages or, as Renaissance people themselves believed, a brilliant new age, there can be little doubt that it was a time of great accomplishment and change.

Far left: *In the Middle Ages, people who challenge accepted beliefs are mistrusted and persecuted. In this medieval painting, a heretic (someone who does not believe the Church's teachings) is burned to death.*
Left: *Even before the Renaissance begins and Brunelleschi develops his mathematical system of perspective, Italian painters are trying to find a way to create a sense of depth in their paintings. In this painting of Christ entering Jerusalem, Duccio di Buoninsegna (c. 1260–1318), a painter from the city of Siena, creates a sense of depth largely through his depiction of architectural features.*
Below: *Most medieval art is religious, and among the most spectacular achievements of the age are cathedrals and churches, built not by one artist but by many craftsmen. Gloucester Cathedral in England is a typical late-medieval cathedral.*

The Humanists

Some historians date the beginning of the Renaissance from the time of the Italian poet and scholar Francesco Petrarca (1304–1374). Petrarch, as he is known to us, was crowned poet laureate in Rome in 1341 and was well known for his essays and letters on historical and philosophical themes as well as for his poems.

Petrarch urged a renewed attention to classical texts and a return to the kind of education that boys received in ancient Rome, which was based on the study of the humanities — Latin language and literature, poetry, history, ethics (correct behavior), and rhetoric (public speaking and elegant expression). He held that such an education developed the whole person, not just the intellect, and prepared one to lead a good and happy life.

In order to learn more about antiquity, humanists investigated the archaeological remains of ancient Italy and searched monastery libraries for ancient documents. They soon realized that in order to pursue their studies they needed to learn Greek, a language then virtually unknown in western Europe. In the 1390s, in order to overcome this obstacle, a group of humanists invited an ambassador from Constantinople named Manuel Chrysoloras to teach Greek in Florence. Later, in the early years of the

15th century, a few Italian humanists traveled to Constantinople and other parts of the Byzantine Empire to bring back original Greek texts. When Constantinople was captured by the Ottoman Turks in 1453, more books arrived with the many Greek scholars who fled to Italy.

The dialogues of the philosopher Plato (*c.* 427–347 B.C.) were among the most influential Greek texts. They so impressed the humanist Marsilio Ficino (1433–1499) and his followers that they declared Plato to be as important as Moses and claimed that Plato had been "a Christian before Christ." Their ideas — for instance, that beauty and love were revelations of God — encouraged Renaissance thinkers and artists to find harmony between classical and Christian beliefs.

Although scholars like Petrarch and Ficino valued the Christian as well as the classical tradition, some people regarded the humanists as troublemakers. Lorenzo Valla

(1407–1457), who wrote an influential textbook on the Latin language, disturbed Church authorities when he used his scholarship to criticize the existing Latin translation of the Bible; when he proved that the Donation of Constantine (a document giving the pope the right to rule central Italy) was a forgery, the pope was furious.

Many humanists are employed as tutors for the children of Italian rulers and nobles.

Above left: The Birth of Venus *by the Florentine painter Sandro Botticelli (1444–1510) shows the beautiful Greek goddess of love, Venus, being reborn out of the formless sea, just as the humanists imagine civilization is being reborn after the chaos of the Middle Ages.*

Below: *An imaginary meeting of four of Florence's leading humanists, painted by Domenico Ghirlandaio (1449–1494) as a detail in a larger painting. The figures are said to be Marsilio Ficino, the Latin scholar and poet Cristoforo Landino (1424–1492), the poet Politian (Angelo Poliziano; 1454–1494), and Demetrios Chalkondylas, professor of Greek at the Academy in Florence.*

Humanism Wins a City

For 12 years, from 1390 to 1402, the republican city-state of Florence was forced to fight for its freedom in a war with Gian Galeazzo Visconti, the duke of nearby Milan, who aspired to rule all of northern Italy. The chancellor of Florence during those years was the humanist scholar Coluccio Salutati (1331–1406). In a series of brilliant letters sent to leaders throughout Italy, Salutati condemned Gian Galeazzo and portrayed Florence as a new Roman republic fighting for freedom against tyranny.

Eventually, in 1402, Gian Galeazzo fell ill and died. Florence had survived. Many Florentines felt that they owed their survival in part to Salutati's inspiring letters. Because Salutati had borrowed examples and stylistic techniques from the Romans, this seemed to prove the value of republicanism and humanism. Classical learning gained new prestige. Humanist ideas were enthusiastically adopted by the nobles and wealthy merchants of the city, and many humanists were appointed as city officials and teachers.

"Florence is the home of the cleverest people. Whatever they do, they do it better than other men, be it warfare, politics, study, philosophy, or trade," writes the scholar Leonardo Bruni (1370–1444). "Civic" humanism — which stresses the importance of a classical education for public leaders and promotes the idea that it is each citizen's duty to act for the common good — develops in Florence. Pride in their city leads Florentines to fund building projects and to commission works of art.

In 1401, the sculptor Lorenzo Ghiberti (1378–1455) wins a competition to design and make the bronze panels for the north doors of the Baptistery, a building set aside for baptisms (above). The doors take him 21 years to complete. Soon after, he is asked to make the east doors; these take him 27 more years to design, cast, and finish (main picture), but they are, according to the artist Michelangelo (1475–1564), "worthy of the gates of paradise."

Florentine Wealth and Patronage

The businesses of Florence were organized into 21 *arti* (guilds). These were associations of craftsmen or merchants that had strict rules intended to maintain high standards of work. The wealthiest was the *Arte di Calimala* (the guild of cloth merchants). At the peak of the city's prosperity, Florentine cloth merchants produced 70,000 pieces of fine material dyed in brilliant yellows and reds every year; each piece was stamped with the seal of the *arte,* which was recognized throughout Europe as a guarantee of quality. There were six other major *arti:* the wool merchants, silk weavers, bankers, lawyers, spice merchants, and fur traders. The members of these guilds were so prosperous, they were nicknamed "the fat people."

The vast majority of the more than 100,000 people who lived in Florence, however, were poor. There were never more than 6,000 members of the 21 *arti,* and most of these people were small craftsmen nicknamed "the thin people" who had little money to spare.

It was the wealth of the fat people that paid for the cultural achievements of the period; their patronage (financial support) enabled artists and scholars to flourish. Why did they spend so much money on the arts? The Church taught that it was evil to profit by lending money or trading, so many merchants felt sinful and tried to earn God's forgiveness by public patronage. Humanists also encouraged the wealthy to spend money for the public benefit, but for other reasons: Leonardo Bruni, recalling ancient Roman ideals, exhorted Florentines to pursue "magnificence" and "glory" in public life regardless of expense.

Civic pride and duty perhaps influenced the *Calimala,* for instance, and led them to accept responsibility for the upkeep of the Baptistery and to commission Ghiberti in 1401. Santa Maria del Fiore, the cathedral of Florence, was the responsibility of the wool guild; it commissioned the architect Filippo Brunelleschi to build the cathedral's dome. The wealthy Florentine merchant and banker Cosimo de' Medici (1389–1464) poured money into the building of churches; he spent more than 40,000 florins on rebuilding the convent of San Marco in Florence (in periods of scarcity, one florin

might buy about ten pounds of pork).

Books and things of beauty also gave a wealthy patron an opportunity to escape from the violence and suffering of everyday life. In addition to founding the Platonic Academy in Florence and supporting humanist scholars including Marsilio Ficino, Cosimo built for himself Roman-style villas in the countryside and decorated them with frescoes (a type of painting made directly on walls) and statues. His grandson Lorenzo the Magnificent (1449–1492) collected Greek and Roman antiquities and invited humanists and artists to discuss philosophy at his table. He lavished money on festivals and tournaments, employing a host of artists to make the masks, banners, and floats. Lorenzo, who had been edu-

cated by humanist teachers, said that learning provided relaxation at those times "when my mind is disturbed by the tumult of public affairs."

Important men also used patronage to flaunt their wealth and demonstrate or justify their power. The Medici, for example, unofficially ruled Florence for much of the 15th century although they were not nobles and their power was not justified by a hereditary title. By spending so much on their city and its culture, the Medici may have hoped to show that they deserved to rule.

Artists often include their patrons in their paintings. Among the Wise Men in The Procession of the Magi *(painted for the chapel of the Medici palace), the artist Benozzo Gozzoli (1420–1497) includes (on a white horse) the young Lorenzo de' Medici. Following him, also on horseback, are his father, Piero, and his grandfather Cosimo. Because he is working for the wealthy Medici, Benozzo is able to use gold in this painting as well as a blue paint made from crushed gemstones.*
Above left: *The Medici family's Villa di Castello.*
Right: *European traders use a coin that contains 10 ounces (3.5 grams) of gold as currency. Coins minted in Venice are known as ducats; coins minted in Florence are known as florins.*

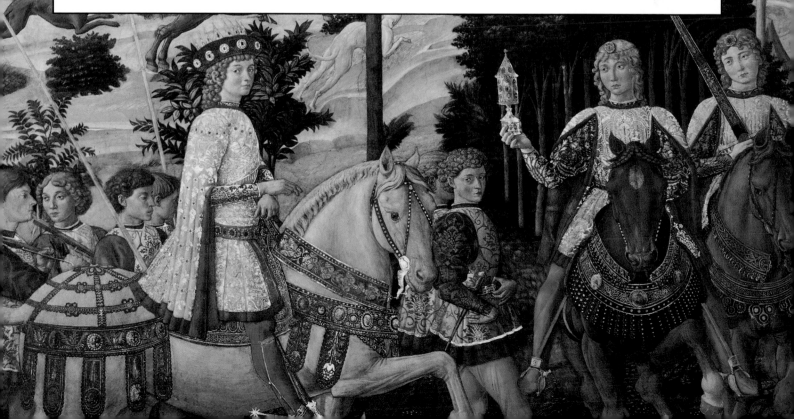

Painting in Perspective

An important new technique that distinguished many Renaissance paintings from earlier medieval paintings was the use of perspective. Sometime after 1410, the architect Filippo Brunelleschi worked out a new way to depict three-dimensional objects or scenes on a two-dimensional (flat) surface. Brunelleschi called his method perspective; using it, artists could make their paintings look more realistic than medieval art.

Brunelleschi had noticed that the parallel stripes of green marble on the angled sides of the Baptistery in Florence seemed to get closer together the farther away they were

from the viewer. He developed a mathematical system whereby an artist could convincingly re-create this effect on a flat surface to give the illusion of distance. Brunelleschi's ideas became well known after the architect Leon Battista Alberti (1404–1472) published them in 1435 in his book *On Painting*.

One of the first artists to use the new technique was the Florentine painter Masaccio (Tommaso di Giovanni; 1401–1428). The most enthusiastic student of the new ideas, however, was another Florentine painter, Paolo Uccello (1397–1475). Ac-

cording to legend, when his wife suggested he come to bed, he said he preferred to stay with his "sweet mistress, perspective."

An artist uses a screen known as Alberti's veil to get the correct perspective for his drawing of a lute. He has drawn a grid to correspond to the veil, and now he copies what he sees, square by square. To give the illusion of depth, he shortens the lines projecting away from the onlooker; this technique is known as foreshortening.
Left: *In his sketch (c. 1481) for the background of the painting* The Adoration of the Magi *(unfinished), Leonardo da Vinci imagines a "vanishing point" on the horizon (behind the rearing horse in the center) and projects all the lines of the drawing to this single point. In this way, he creates a scene that seems to have three dimensions.*

Architecture: New and Ancient

Classical Greek and Roman architecture fascinated Renaissance architects. Because many buildings had survived from Roman times (for instance, the Pantheon and the Colosseum in Rome), builders as well as humanist historians were able to study these structures in an attempt to better understand classical building techniques.

Filippo Brunelleschi had never built a dome before he agreed to design one for the cathedral in Florence in 1418. He had, however, read books by the Roman architect Vitruvius and had studied ancient Roman buildings, even to the point of climbing onto their roofs and taking off the tiles. Some thought that building a dome large enough to fit the cathedral was impossible, but Brunelleschi was sure he would be able to overcome the difficulties of the project.

Brunelleschi's contemporary biographer reports that when the committee appointed by the wool guild to select a builder for the dome asked Brunelleschi to explain the methods he intended to use, he refused. When the committee insisted, he grew abusive and was carried from the room. Still, the committee gave him the assignment (according to this account, when he completed

a smaller dome using his innovative ideas). After 16 years' work, the dome, which became a model for all future domed buildings, was completed.

Other Renaissance architects soon began to imitate many aspects of Brunelleschi's work. The art historian Giorgio Vasari (1511–1574) went so far as to claim that Brunelleschi had been "sent by heaven to give architecture new forms, after it had wandered astray for many centuries."

Many architects copy the features of the church of San Lorenzo in Florence, designed by Brunelleschi. His design follows classical principles; it is based on the circle and the square, and the different parts of the building are proportioned according to mathematical ratios (notably 1:2:5). He also uses Greek-style Corinthian columns. **Above:** *The Temple of Neptune at Paestum, an ancient Greek colony in southern Italy, is one of many buildings that architects like Brunelleschi study.*

Sculpture

Like architects, early Renaissance sculptors studied and imitated ancient Roman forms. Following classical models, they made equestrian monuments (statues of riders on horseback) and busts of famous people.

Andrea del Verrocchio (1436–1488) was typical of many of the sculptors of the early Renaissance. One of the most influential artists of his time, he worked in his *bottega* (workshop), helped by his assistants and apprentices. Under Verrocchio, the *bottega* produced a range of works for Florentine merchants and nobles, including statues, busts, pictures, chairs, plates, goblets, and even a ceremonial suit of armor. Verrocchio was not wealthy; his tax return for 1457 claimed that he was not earning enough to buy hose (stockings) for his workers.

During the early years of the Renaissance, artists were still primarily considered craftsmen, as they had been in the Middle Ages. Because of the materials they used, sculptors often belonged to the stonemasons' guild while painters belonged to the guild of doctors and apothecaries. But

some ancient authors whom the humanists studied said that artists were divinely inspired, and the spread of humanism encouraged changes in society's ideas about artists. By the end of the 14th century, Florentine painters had been recognized as having "great importance in the life of the state"; later in the Renaissance, individual artists would achieve fame and high social standing.

The Roman statue of Emperor Marcus Aurelius (far left) provides an example for both a statue of the Paduan military leader Gattamelata by Donatello (Donato Bardi; 1386–1466) (below left) and a statue of the Venetian general Colleoni by Verrocchio (below). Such statues reflect the new influence of classical forms and the increasing emphasis on the individual as a subject for art.
Right: *Donatello's David, cast in bronze (c. 1430) for the Medici palace courtyard, carries an inscription on its base that states that David is a symbol of Florentine liberty (Florence being a small but victorious David opposed to a powerful Goliath, Milan).*

A Painter at Work

Fresco, a method of painting known since Roman times, had a particular appeal for Renaissance painters. Cennino Cennini, author of *The Craftsman's Handbook* (1390), described it as "the sweetest, most attractive way of working there is." Making a fresco involves painting directly onto a newly plastered wall with a mixture of pure pigment and lime water. As the artist works, the lime in the wet plaster mixes with the paint and reacts with the carbon dioxide in the air, forming a hard, permanent surface. The colors this technique produces seem translucent and shining.

Considerable skill is involved in creating a fresco. The artist has to complete the work before the plaster dries (the Italian word *fresco* means "fresh"). A mistake can be corrected only by waiting until the plaster has set, chipping it off, and starting again.

High up on scaffolding, the Renaissance artist would concentrate on the difficult parts of the painting while his apprentices brought more paint or worked on less complicated sections. More than one artist was said to have fallen to his death in the confusion.

Below, top left: *The first step when painting a fresco is to plaster the wall. Sometimes artists cover the wall with matting made from woven, flattened cane in an attempt to stop damp from coming through later. Two layers of plaster are applied to the wall to give a thick, flat, absorbent base for the fresco. Onto this the artist will sketch a rough design in a brownish red pigment. The sketch,*

called a sinopia, *gives the patron an idea of what the finished fresco will look like.*

Opposite, bottom left: *When the artist is ready, an apprentice makes the paints. This highly skilled task involves grinding together metal oxides, minerals such as ocher, and many other substances such as berries, flowers, and insects. Meanwhile, another workman puts a thin top layer of plaster over a patch of wall (the giornata). Because the paint must be applied to wet plaster, he covers only as much of the wall or ceiling as the artist can paint in a single day (giornata means "a day's work," roughly equivalent to six to eight hours). The size of the giornata varies from day to day according to how much time-consuming detail the artist has to paint in a particular section of the fresco.*

Opposite, top right: *Most artists prepare cartoons (drawings on paper) in their studios and set their apprentices to prick hundreds of tiny holes around the outlines of the drawings. Before they start to paint, they place the cartoon over the wet plaster. A muslin bag containing pigment is pressed against the holes in the cartoon; the pigment goes through, onto the wet plaster.*

Opposite, bottom right: *The artist then joins the dots, creating an outline to follow as he paints the fresco.*

Above: *The artist paints quickly from top to bottom of the giornata. Because blue pigment turns green when combined with lime, the sky will be added a secco (when the plaster is dry). Details such as buttons and jewelry can also be added when the fresco has dried; paint applied to dry plaster, however, often peels off later.*

A New Approach to Art

Breaking away from the medieval custom of painting mainly religious scenes, Renaissance artists turned their energies to portraits, a genre of painting almost forgotten in the Middle Ages but much in demand among Renaissance patrons. They also began to paint scenes from history and from the Greek and Roman myths that so interested humanists. One historian has calculated that while only one in 20 paintings in the 1420s was of a secular (nonreligious) nature, by the 1520s one in five had a secular subject.

In addition, artists made a number of technical advances during the 15th century. The use of perspective changed the composition of paintings, and painters experimented with new materials. They started to use oil paint, for example, instead of tempera (powdered pigments mixed to a paste with egg yolk), which had been widely used before.

Artists were excited by the new ideas and approaches they had discovered; they felt, as Alberti wrote, that "man can do all things if he will." In this celebratory spirit, Renaissance artists filled their paintings with figures of beautiful women and handsome, muscular men and paid great attention to the settings in which their subjects were placed, filling them with pets, possessions, plants, buildings, and bystanders. Whereas the subjects portrayed in medieval

paintings are solemn, majestic, and often sad, the people in many Renaissance paintings seem to be enjoying life.

Left: Andrea Mantegna (1431–1506) is one of the most important artists of the early Renaissance. His Parnassus *(1497) is inspired by classical mythology. While the nine Muses dance and sing, Venus, the goddess of love, and Mars, the god of war, embrace, causing volcanic eruptions. To the left are Vulcan at his forge and Orpheus playing a lyre. On the right stand Mercury and the winged horse Pegasus, who stamps his hoof to stop the eruptions.*
Below: In a fresco painted on the ceiling of the Camera degli Sposi in the Palazzo Ducale in Mantua (c. 1473), Mantegna uses the technique of foreshortening to create the illusion that the figures are actually standing up or peering down from high above the viewer's head. Those parts of the figures that would be farther away if the scene were real are drawn with proportionally shorter lines than their "closer" parts.
Right: Mantegna is one of the first artists to try to make the details of his paintings historically correct. In Trumpeters, Bearers of Standards, and Banners *(one of a series of paintings called* The Triumphs of Caesar *[c. 1480–1495]), he paints details described by ancient*

Roman authors in their accounts of victory parades: the garlands on the trumpeters' heads, the straight tubing of the trumpets, the paintings of captured cities held up by the standard-bearers, and the statues (though Mantegna probably misunderstood his source when he put them on poles).

Books and Printing

The Renaissance began many years before the first printed books, but printing made the ideas of the Renaissance available to a wider audience. Through printing, large numbers of people were able to do as the humanists recommended — study classical texts.

Before printing, every book had to be copied by hand, usually onto calfskin parchment. Around 1439, however, a citizen of Mainz in Germany named Johann Gutenberg (c. 1399–1468) invented a mechanical printing press. For years, craftsmen had been experimenting with blocks of wood onto which the text of a book was carved. Gutenberg developed the idea of movable metal letters that could be assembled in any order to form the text.

The first printing presses in Italy were set up during the 1460s. At first, people did not like the look of the new printed books, so printers left spaces for scribes to add decorations by hand. Wealthy patrons even employed scribes to make handwritten copies of books that had been printed.

By 1500, however, there were more than 200 printing presses in Venice alone, and the Venetian printer Aldus Manutius (1449–1515) was producing large numbers of classical Greek and Roman texts in pocket-size editions — the Aldine classics. Aldus established the importance of a clear, accurate, easy-to-read text. Because books like the Aldine classics could be produced relatively cheaply, scholars could more easily find and study the texts. In fact, as books became readily obtainable, men and women who wished to appear cultured had little excuse if they were not well read.

In mechanical printing, the letters are assembled in a form (frame) and inked with an inkball (top left). After placing a sheet of paper over the form, a workman pulls the lever of the printing press to press the paper onto the type (main picture). After a moment, the workman releases the lever and lifts the printed page from the form (left center). Printing offers people greater access to books like the Bible. This Bible (bottom left) was printed by Johann Gutenberg in 1455.

The Courts of Italy

Unlike Florence, most Italian states were not republics; they were ruled by "princes" — kings, dukes, marquises, and counts. These rulers, often enemies on the battlefield, vied with each other in their courts to appear cultured and modern, employing the best artists and writers of the time. Their patronage enabled art and scholarship to flourish throughout Italy. In Naples, for example, King Alfonso I (ruled 1442–1458) read the books of the Roman authors Livy and Seneca every day and spent the vast sum of 20,000 ducats a year supporting humanist scholars.

MANTUA, FERRARA, AND RIMINI

In Mantua, the marquis Gianfrancesco Gonzaga (ruled 1407–1444) invited the great humanist teacher Vittorino da Feltre (1378–1446) to set up a school for the children of the nobility. Vittorino believed that

school ought to be enjoyable; he called his school the Pleasant House. He accepted girls as pupils and admitted a few children from poor families who did not have to pay to be educated alongside Gianfrancesco's son Ludovico.

In the tiny duchy of Ferrara, the Este family patronized important Renaissance artists. Leonello d'Este (ruled 1441–1450) commissioned buildings by the architect Alberti and frescoes by the artist Mantegna.

He apparently applied ideas of refined taste to the details of life as well; a contemporary reports that he dressed tastefully, without great display, choosing the colors of his garments according to "the day of the month and the position of the stars and planets." Under Duke Ercole d'Este (ruled 1471–1505), Ferrara became a center of poetry and drama. The poet Ludovico Ariosto (1474–1533) was employed there as a diplomat. His influential epic poem *Orlando Furioso* ("Mad Roland") celebrated the Este family, comparing its members to the heroes of ancient legends.

Like other princes, the ruler of the papal territory of Rimini, Sigismondo Malatesta (ruled 1432–1468), accumulated wealth by hiring out his army to whomever could pay. At home, Sigismondo spent generously on the arts, employing humanists to write poems celebrating his military successes as well as his love for his wife, Isotta. He commissioned Alberti to redesign the church of San Francesco in Rimini in the style of a classical temple. Known as the Tempio Malatestiano, it is richly decorated with sculptures of pagan gods, signs of the zodiac, the Malatesta coat of arms, and the magnificent tombs of Sigismondo and Isotta.

MILAN

In Milan, the powerful Sforza family supported humanist writers and had their children educated by humanist teachers. During the time of Duke Ludovico Sforza (ruled 1494–1500) and his wife, Beatrice d'Este, daughter of Ferrara's Duke Ercole d'Este, Milan became a center for the study of Greek and Latin. According to Beatrice's secretary, "the court was full of men of every skill and talent, especially poets and musicians, and no month passed without some production or play." One of the artists employed at the court was Leonardo da Vinci, who had applied for the position of military engineer there. While in Milan, Leonardo painted *The Last Supper* (1495–1497). He also designed complicated stage sets to help the court celebrate weddings and other occasions. For one of the court masques (dramatic entertainments), Leonardo designed a giant hemisphere, painted and set with torches to represent the night sky. According to an observer of the performance, actors representing the planets moved within the hemisphere, aided by machinery and accompanied by music. At the climax, the actors descended to the stage to praise the couple of honor.

URBINO

Remarkably, one of the major centers of the Renaissance was the tiny duchy of Urbino. In the mountains of central Italy, Urbino was one of the states that owed allegiance to the pope. It was less than 40 miles (64 kilometers) square, but it developed into perhaps the most refined of all the Renaissance courts.

Duke Frederigo da Montefeltro (ruled 1444–1482; his first name is sometimes spelled Frederico) was educated at Vittorino's school in Mantua. He seems to have been the model of a cultured Renaissance prince. According to his librarian and biographer, the duke was very religious; he attended mass twice a day and forbade swearing and gambling at court. He maintained a household of 500 people, including four humanist teachers, five architects, five engineers, four transcribers of manuscripts, and five readers who read the works of Livy aloud during meals.

Duke Frederigo employed the architect Francesco Laurana (*c.* 1430–1502) "to make our city of Urbino a beautiful residence worthy of . . . our own status" and spent a fortune on the arts, bringing painters and tapestry makers from Flanders. His library — on which he spent 30,000 ducats — contained copies of all the Greek, Latin, and Hebrew texts then known, books on Church history and theology, and a complete series of works by Italian poets as well as books on mathematics, music, military tactics, and the arts. In times of scarcity, he bought grain for the poor and lent money to shopkeepers who had got into difficulties. "I am not a merchant. It is enough to have saved my people from hunger," he is said to have commented.

Left: A fresco painted by Mantegna in 1472 shows the family of Ludovico Gonzaga of Mantua (ruled 1444–1478).

Below: Frederigo da Montefeltro of Urbino with his son Guidobaldo. Frederigo continues to have books copied by hand long after printing is commonplace; each volume is bound in red leather embossed with silver.

The Courtier

The court at Urbino, as it was in 1506 or 1507, was idealized by the writer Baldassare Castiglione (1478–1529) in his book *The Courtier* (published 1528). By 1506, Duke Frederigo had been succeeded by his son Guidobaldo (ruled 1482–1508). According to Castiglione, the young duke possessed "as well as a friendly and charming nature, an infinite range of knowledge." His wife, Elisabetta Gonzaga (1471–1526), who was from Mantua, had such modesty and nobility that "those seeing her for the first time realized that she was a very great lady." Around them gathered a large group of courtiers (members of the inner circle of the duke's friends); they were all "very noble and worthy gentlemen . . . poets, musicians, buffoons of all kinds, and the finest talent of every description anywhere in Italy." Among them were the painter Giovanni Santi (died 1494), whose son Raphael (1483–1520) later became one of the best-known painters of the Renaissance; and of course, Castiglione himself, who stayed in Urbino from 1505 to 1508.

Days at the court of Urbino, said Castiglione, were spent in "honorable and pleasing

activities of the body and the mind," such as tournaments, riding, games, and musical performances. At night, the ladies and gentlemen of the court amused themselves by taking part in intellectual debates.

The Courtier describes a series of these discussions, including one on the topic, What makes the ideal courtier?

Talking long into the night, Duke Guidobaldo's courtiers and guests detail the attributes of the perfect courtier. He must be a "universal man." Culture, grace and refinement, noble birth, courage on the battlefield, and sporting ability are vital. He must be educated and articulate. He should show a knowledge of the classics and be able to understand art and sculpture. Singing and dancing are es-

sential skills. He must eat politely, without making noises by grinding or sucking his teeth. He must be witty; practical jokes are acceptable, but it is important not to go too far. A great deal of time is spent discussing servants and clothes; a man with very fat or very thin legs should not draw attention to them by wearing brightly colored hose. The good courtier must be modest and should make his achievements seem effortless, but at the same time, he must make sure that his virtues are seen. Finally, he must be unquestioningly loyal to his prince.

Two poets, two musicians, and a sculptor take part in the discussions, alongside the courtiers, state officials, soldiers, and visiting nobles. In the middle of the 15th century, most artists belonged to the craftsman class. Donatello, for example, was the son of a wool-comber, and when Cosimo de' Medici gave him a red cloak (a rich man's garment), he declined to wear it. Now, however, artists have risen in status and are accepted in the upper classes of society.

Renaissance Women

Another topic that the courtiers at Urbino addressed in their discussions was the nature and proper place of women. According to Castiglione, one of the men, Giuliano de' Medici (1479–1516), declared that "all of us know that it is fitting for the courtier to have the greatest reverence for women . . . a serious woman, strengthened by virtue and insight, acts as a shield against the insolence and beastliness of arrogant men." The ideal Renaissance gentleman, according to Giuliano, showed respect to women. Another man, Ottaviano Fregoso (1470–1524), seems to have disagreed. He declared women to be "very imperfect creatures, of little or no dignity compared with men, and incapable in themselves of performing any good act."

Fregoso's was a commonly held opinion throughout the Renaissance, as it had been in the Middle Ages. A sign at the gate of a public garden in Florence read: ENTRY FORBIDDEN TO GEESE, WOMEN, AND GOATS. Young girls were often kept shut up at home or in convents. At a marriageable age — sometimes as young as eight or ten years old — they were "sold," on their father's instructions, to a suitable man who would make a good ally for the family.

There is evidence, however, that at least in refined Renaissance society the status of women improved. Women such as Beatrice and Isabella d'Este were educated and came to play an important role in intellectual life. A number of women, such as Antonia Uccello (the daughter of the Florentine painter Paolo Uccello), became successful artists, and there were several female humanists and poets. Most women were not

part of court society, but there was no doubt that the women at the court of Urbino were not inferior; the discussions were led by the duchess Elisabetta and her friend Emilia Pia (died 1528). One night, at a nod from the duchess, the ladies of the court even playfully attacked one of the male guests whose comments about women seemed to them far too negative.

During the Renaissance, women could inherit full legal title to their husbands' property; because they typically married men several years older than themselves, the chances of this happening increased. A wealthy widow named Alessandra Macinghi Strozzi filled her letters to her son with details about her life as a landowner — her difficulties paying taxes, her plans for the next harvest, her struggles with her peasants, her efforts to provide a dowry for her daughter, and the care she took in teaching a young son how to write. In 1500, Caterina Sforza (c. 1463–1509), who had become ruler of the town of Forlì when her husband died, defended it fiercely against the military leader Cesare Borgia (1476–1507) until all was lost.

Many women from wealthy families are well educated. A few, like Dorotea Bucca (1400–1436), who becomes a lecturer in medicine at the University of Bologna, even manage to have successful careers as scholars.
Right: *A self-portrait by Sofonisba Anguissola, whose father, unusually, apprentices her to an artist, thus preparing her for a career as a portrait painter that will include 20 years at the court of the king of Spain.*

Violence and Intrigue

It is remarkable that the refined court life and tremendous creativity of the Renaissance took place against a background of war and violence. For the first half of the 15th century, until the treaty of the Peace of Lodi (1454), the states of Italy were constantly at war. Each state employed *condottieri* (hired soldiers) to attack the others. Even that paragon of virtue, Duke Frederigo of Urbino, made his fortune by selling his services as a soldier to the governments of other Italian states.

The princes of the tiny Italian states were notoriously vicious. There was no common understanding, as there is today, that rulers have a duty to ensure the well-being of their subjects. Most Italian princes were mainly concerned with staying in power, as some popular stories show. King Ferrante of Naples governed his kingdom through terror and violence. He embalmed the bodies of those opponents he had put to death, keeping them as gruesome trophies and a warning to others. Duke Galeazzo Maria Sforza of Milan (ruled 1466–1476), who was obsessed with the beauty of his own hands and voice, humiliated his prisoners by forcing them to eat excrement. Eventually, he himself was stabbed to death by three assassins at the end of a church service. In 1494, his brother Ludovico Sforza gained control of Milan by poisoning his nephew. In Ferrara, Ercole d'Este poisoned his wife when he thought she was conspiring against him. These were the same rulers who were pouring money into humanist studies and exquisite works of art.

In about 1516, Niccolò Machiavelli (1469–1527), a former chancellor of Florence, wrote *The Prince* for Lorenzo the Magnificent's grandson, also called Lorenzo, who was duke of Urbino from 1516 to 1519. The book advised the young duke about how to survive in such a world. The advice was candid and harsh: Although it might be beneficial to seem to be a good man, it is better to be feared than loved; successful rulers are ruthless; the best security is a strong army; and a wise ruler destroys his people's freedom before they destroy him. Force, fraud, and broken promises are acceptable, claims Machiavelli, as long as they keep the ruler in power.

In this painting by Giovanni Bellini (c. 1430–1516), woodcutters ignore an assassination; the painting suggests that violence is so common it is unremarkable. **Right:** *The brutal punishments for even relatively minor offenses such as burglary include torture, burning, and hanging — as shown in this painting by Pisanello (Antonio Pisano; c. 1395–1455).*

The Papacy

During the Renaissance, as in the Middle Ages, the Catholic Church, led by the pope, was the central spiritual authority in the lives of western Europeans. At the same time, the Church ruled the Papal States, a belt of land across the center of Italy. In many ways, the Vatican palace in Rome functioned very much like any other Italian court.

Like other Renaissance princes, the popes often used their wealth and power for patronage. Pope Nicholas V (reigned 1447–1455) was the first humanist pope. He was an able scholar who employed Alberti to rebuild bridges and the Vergine aqueduct in Rome. His collection of 9,000 books and manuscripts formed the basis of the Vatican library, and he advised both Cosimo de' Medici and Frederigo of Urbino about how to set up their libraries. Sixtus IV (reigned 1471–1484) also patronized numerous artists, including Ghirlandaio, Botticelli, and Mantegna, and undertook important projects, including the building of the Sistine Chapel in the Vatican.

Some of the popes, including Sixtus and one of his successors, Alexander VI (reigned 1492–1503), also shared the faults of the worst Renaissance princes. Sixtus was corrupt, promoting family and friends to important Church positions—he even made one of his servants, an uneducated 20-year-old man, bishop of Parma in 1463. In 1478, Sixtus supported a plot to assassinate Lorenzo the Magnificent and his brother Giuliano during mass. When the hired cutthroat, who had begun to admire Lorenzo, refused to do the deed, the conspirators recruited two willing priests.

Writing of Alexander, Machiavelli commented that "he never did anything else but tell lies . . . and break promises." In Rome, Alexander lived in the greatest luxury. His mistress was only 14 when he seduced her away from her husband. When he became pope, he installed her in rooms next to St. Peter's Church in the Vatican so that he could visit her through a secret door. Rome was scandalized when he had her portrait painted, as the Virgin Mary, on his bedroom wall.

Alexander loaded honors upon his son Cesare Borgia. Cesare was an able commander, but he was violent and treacherous. His military campaigns to reduce the nobles of the Papal States to obedience (1499–1503) were so ruthless that they led Machiavelli to use Cesare as the model for his ideal prince.

By contrast, Alexander's successor, Julius II (reigned 1503–1513), is remembered for commissioning some of the greatest triumphs of Renaissance art. Julius persuaded Michelangelo to paint the Sistine Chapel and employed Raphael to paint his rooms in the Vatican. At Julius's request, the architect Donato Bramante (Donato Lazzari; 1444–1514) made plans to rebuild St. Peter's Cathedral in Rome, construction on which began during Julius's reign.

Julius was an accomplished military leader as well as a generous patron. He himself led an army to defend Italy against a French invasion that began in 1511. In 1513, his forces succeeded in driving the invaders out. Julius's idea of freeing all of Italy (not just his own Papal States) from French domination was "well in advance of most political thinking of the day."

A cardinal places the papal crown on the head of the pope, who carries a crook symbolizing his position as shepherd of the Catholic Church.

The pope claims to speak with the authority of God when he speaks ex cathedra *(from his throne). Some people, however, are shocked by the behavior of popes such as Alexander and view the involvement of the popes in secular affairs critically. The Dutch humanist Desiderius Erasmus (c. 1469–1536) calls the papacy the "disease of Christendom," and Lorenzo the Magnificent accuses Rome of being a "sink of all vices."*

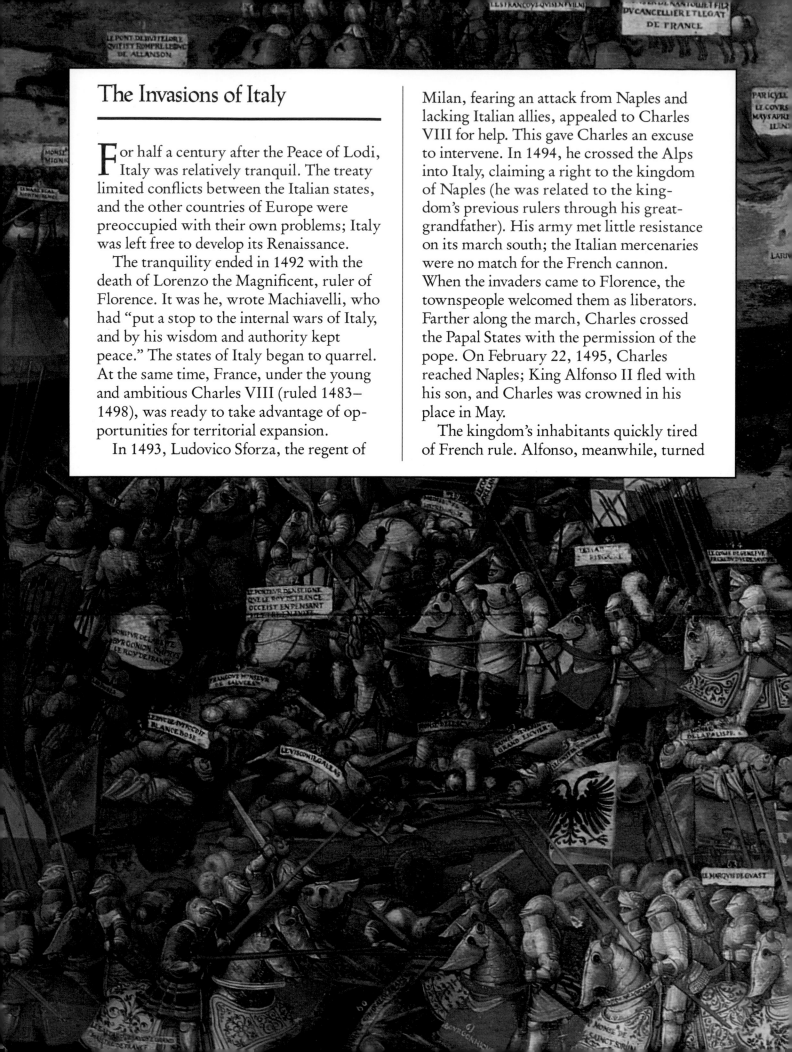

The Invasions of Italy

For half a century after the Peace of Lodi, Italy was relatively tranquil. The treaty limited conflicts between the Italian states, and the other countries of Europe were preoccupied with their own problems; Italy was left free to develop its Renaissance.

The tranquility ended in 1492 with the death of Lorenzo the Magnificent, ruler of Florence. It was he, wrote Machiavelli, who had "put a stop to the internal wars of Italy, and by his wisdom and authority kept peace." The states of Italy began to quarrel. At the same time, France, under the young and ambitious Charles VIII (ruled 1483–1498), was ready to take advantage of opportunities for territorial expansion.

In 1493, Ludovico Sforza, the regent of Milan, fearing an attack from Naples and lacking Italian allies, appealed to Charles VIII for help. This gave Charles an excuse to intervene. In 1494, he crossed the Alps into Italy, claiming a right to the kingdom of Naples (he was related to the kingdom's previous rulers through his great-grandfather). His army met little resistance on its march south; the Italian mercenaries were no match for the French cannon. When the invaders came to Florence, the townspeople welcomed them as liberators. Farther along the march, Charles crossed the Papal States with the permission of the pope. On February 22, 1495, Charles reached Naples; King Alfonso II fled with his son, and Charles was crowned in his place in May.

The kingdom's inhabitants quickly tired of French rule. Alfonso, meanwhile, turned to Spain for help. Spain had been united through the marriage of Ferdinand of Aragon to Isabella of Castile in 1469 and the conquest of Granada in 1492; like France, it was emerging as a major power. Ferdinand sent an army to assist Alfonso in regaining control of Naples. In addition, he formed a league with the pope, the Holy Roman Emperor, and the cities of Milan and Venice against Charles. Charles, still in Italy with his army, had to fight his way back to France. Behind him, all the territories he had conquered were lost.

Italy remained a theater of war until 1559. The French fought major wars there in the years 1499 to 1503, 1511 to 1513, and 1515 to 1516. Spain continued to fight as well, sometimes with the French, sometimes against them.

In this tangle of shifting alliances, the cost in human suffering was clear. Cities were sacked and their inhabitants massacred. There were typhus epidemics in 1505 and 1528, and in the 1520s, there was an outbreak of the plague. Despite these disasters, the arts continued to flourish in Italy and the period from 1495 to 1527 later came to be known as the High Renaissance.

For years, Italy serves as a battleground for the wars of foreign powers. At the Battle of Pavia in 1525, the forces of Charles I of Castile and Aragon (ruled 1516–1556), who became the Holy Roman Emperor Charles V in 1519, defeat the French armies and capture the French king, François I (ruled 1515–1547). **Right:** *An Italian mercenary (hired soldier).*

Leonardo da Vinci

The art historian Kenneth Clark has called Leonardo da Vinci "the most relentlessly curious man in history." The interests that found a home in Leonardo's mind were so numerous and diverse, it was as if all humanity's desire to learn had been concentrated in one person.

Leonardo began his career as an apprentice to the Florentine sculptor Andrea del Verrocchio, who once asked his pupil to add an angel to a painting he had been working on, called *The Baptism of Christ*. According to legend, after comparing Leonardo's angel to his own work, Verrocchio decided to concentrate on sculpture.

In about 1482, Leonardo went to work

for Ludovico Sforza in Milan. There, in addition to painting, he designed costumes and scenery for court entertainments and drew up plans for irrigation projects and new military machines, including a tank, a huge crossbow, life jackets, and a parachute.

In 1499, Leonardo left Milan for Florence, where he continued to work on numerous ambitious projects, not all of which were successfully completed. Commissioned to paint a huge fresco of the Battle of Anghiari, he decided to try a new paint mixture and a kind of plaster described by the ancient Roman writer Pliny. The result was disastrous—the paint did not dry and the colors ran into each other. Leonardo did not finish the painting, which was later plastered over; a few visiting painters, though, were so impressed by the work in progress that they made sketches of it, which were copied over by others. In this way, *The Battle of Anghiari* influenced many other artists.

Leonardo is a vegetarian, an unusual choice in Renaissance times, and cannot bear to see animals in pain. He believes horses to be almost supernatural and does many detailed drawings of them, often from live models.

In 1493, Leonardo completes a full-size clay model for an equestrian statue in Milan of Ludovico Sforza's father, Francesco (ruled 1450–1466), but Ludovico finds another use for the bronze intended for the statue—making cannons to fight the invading French armies—and the statue is never cast. French gunners ruin the model by using it for target practice. Only Leonardo's preliminary drawings (left) survive from the project.

Art and Science

Although he suffered numerous setbacks, Leonardo da Vinci was renowned in his own time and many artists were influenced by him. His sketches of churches, for example, formed the basis of Bramante's design for the new St. Peter's Church in Rome. Art historians date the period they call the High Renaissance from around 1495, when Leonardo began to paint *The Last Supper* for Ludovico Sforza, and some historians assert that Leonardo da Vinci changed the course not only of art but of the Renaissance.

Leonardo was responsible for several important developments in painting. First, his treatment of light was revolutionary. His knowledge of light allowed him to develop the techniques of *chiaroscuro* (light and shade) and *sfumato* (softening of the edges). Rather than using sharp lines, Leonardo used subtly blended colors and shading to define the outlines of his figures. This gave his paintings the sense of gentleness and mystery that fascinates people who see, for instance, the *Mona Lisa*, which was painted during his stay in Florence.

Leonardo also did detailed research for his paintings. He was not content to depict the outside of things; he wanted to see inside them, to understand why they worked as they did. "Art truly is a science," he explained. He dissected more than ten corpses in order to understand the anatomy of the human body. He filled his notebooks with thousands of pages of sketches and preliminary drawings.

Simple curiosity as well as research for his paintings led Leonardo to conduct what were in fact scientific investigations. His notebooks are packed with left-handed mirror writing describing his observations and discoveries in anatomy, mechanics, hydraulics, geology, and botany. He spent weeks experimenting with flies, trimming their wings or putting honey on them to study how this changed the sound of their buzzing. He made a particular study of the flight of birds. Later, he became obsessed with mathematics. In 1509, he illustrated a

book by the mathematician Luca Pacioli (1445–1517) called *The Divine Proportion*. Pacioli had calculated that the perfect ratio was 1:1.6 and that a rectangle of these proportions was the shape most pleasing to the eye. This concept, which Leonardo renamed the golden section, is still studied by artists and mathematicians.

Leonardo rejected the medieval view of science, which held that nature was controlled by spiritual powers — that, for instance, it was the soul of a bird that allowed it to fly. "A bird is an instrument working according to mathematical law," he wrote. Leonardo insisted that observation and ex-periments were the only way to find out the truth about nature. In this, he can be said to be the founder of modern science.

As a young man, Leonardo wrote, "I wish to work miracles." In his old age, he seems to have felt that he had failed — throughout his notebooks he wrote comments such as "Tell me if anything at all was achieved." But Leonardo's obsession with experimental investigation, though it sometimes led to failure, also marked an important change in the direction of the Renaissance. Before Leonardo, artists and scholars had been content to imitate the Greeks and Romans; in the words of one modern historian, they had tried to "recover the past." After Leonardo da Vinci, during the High Renaissance, artists and scholars sought new knowledge about the unexplored possibilities of their fields.

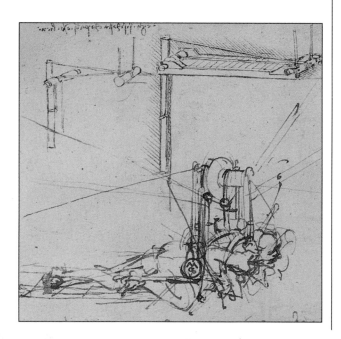

Leonardo's understanding of light and human movement enable him to depict, as he says, "the intention of men's souls." In his fresco The Last Supper, *commissioned by Ludovico Sforza for a monastery dining hall in Milan, for example, he successfully portrays both the guilt of Judas Iscariot and the resignation of Jesus Christ, who accepts his destiny calmly. Unfortunately, Leonardo experiments with a mixture of oil and tempera that begins to flake off the plaster within a few years of the fresco's completion.*
Far left: Leonardo's angel in The Virgin of the Rocks *(c. 1506) illustrates his mastery of the techniques of* chiaroscuro *(light and shade) and* sfumato *(softening of the edges).*
Left: The flying machine sketched in Leonardo's notebook anticipates a modern hang glider.

The Roman Renaissance

According to a modern historian, during the 15th century the city of Rome became "the center of Western civilization." The popes lived in Rome, which made the city the administrative center of the Catholic Church. From all over western Europe, Church taxes flowed into Rome. The city became a diplomatic center, and its bankers flourished. Finally, during the reign of Pope Julius II, Rome replaced Florence as the center of the Renaissance.

The popes were great patrons of the arts. Julius commissioned some of the most important works of Raphael and Michelangelo. The reign of his successor, Leo X (reigned 1513–1521), is often called the golden age of the Renaissance because of Leo's investment in cultural projects.

Leo was the son of Lorenzo the Magnificent. On becoming pope, he allegedly told a friend: "Let us enjoy the papacy." He supported a vast number of poets, artists, and scholars, and spent 8,000 ducats a month on presents for his favorites (and on gambling). He set up a school of Greek in Rome, and he expanded the university until it had more than 100 teachers.

Leo loved music. When he became pope, many of the singers in Mantua left for Rome to seek his patronage. He employed 15 composers, including the lute player Gian Maria Giuldeo, who was paid 23 ducats a month and raised to the rank of count.

A major rebuilding program was started in Rome during the time of Leo X. The Vatican was extended and lavishly redecorated. Leo also had much of Rome's old medieval housing knocked down to create large squares and afford a better view of the surviving Roman architecture. He spent so much that he emptied the papal treasury, and when he died owing 622,000 ducats, he almost ruined the bankers of Rome.

Meanwhile, the cardinals of the Church and Roman bankers such as the papal treasurer Agostino Chigi (1465–1520) poured money into art and architecture. Thousands of workers came to Rome from Milan to build cardinals' palaces, merchants' mansions, and new churches. Whereas in 1503 there had been only eight painters living in the city of Rome, in 1528, the Fraternity of St. Luke (the guild of painters in the city) had 124 members.

In Rome, bankers, nobles, and churchmen live extravagantly. One Roman uses silver plates, ostentatiously throwing them into the River Tiber after each course. Unknown to his guests, he has placed a net on the riverbed so he can recover the plates.

Here, during a lavish meal, the pope discusses a commission with an artist. The pope's food taster (who samples his food to make sure it has not been poisoned) stands behind him.

Michelangelo

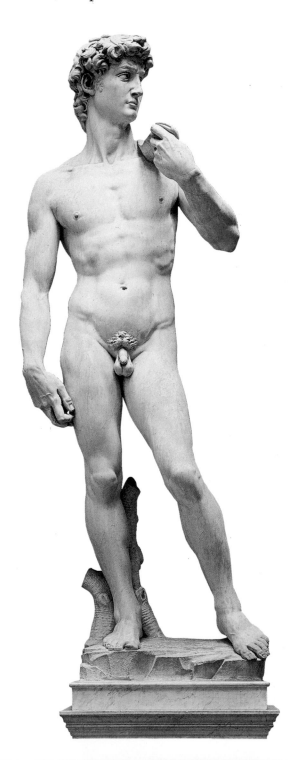

Even during his own lifetime, "the divine Michelangelo" — sculptor, painter, architect, and poet — was held to be a genius. Michelangelo Buonarroti's character fulfills our stereotype of a genius: brilliant yet difficult, outspoken, and unstable. He was often disheveled, and he slept in his boots. He criticized other artists. Once he was so rude that an apprentice punched him and broke his nose. On another occasion, Leonardo da Vinci asked Michelangelo to explain a passage of poetry to some admirers. "Explain it yourself," snapped Michelangelo. He cared little for the wishes of his patrons, and he often put a clause in his contracts that gave him the right to do the work "as it pleases the said Michelangelo." Once, when the pope would not see him, Michelangelo left Rome for seven months. According to the artist, when the pope asked why he had left, Michelangelo replied, "Not from ill will, but from scorn."

Michelangelo learned his skills while apprenticed to the painter Ghirlandaio in Florence. He sketched classical statues in the Medici gardens and imitated them so successfully that his sculpture of a sleeping Cupid was sold by a dealer as an antique.

Like Leonardo da Vinci, Michelangelo changed the way artists viewed their work. Although he understood the rules of perspective and foreshortening, for example, he demanded the right to ignore them when he wanted to create a particular effect in a painting. "All the reasoning of geometry and arithmetic and all the proofs of perspective are of no use to a man without the eye," he remarked. After he had carved the tomb of Giuliano de' Medici (1534), it was observed that the figure on the tomb did not look like the dead man. "A thousand years from now, nobody will want to know what he really looked like," retorted Michelangelo. Out of this attitude came a new style of painting that art historians call mannerism; mannerists strove to define their own styles, even when that meant discarding the realistic depiction of nature.

Michelangelo was an example of the Renaissance universal man; his talents were broad ranging. He wrote poetry in a neat Renaissance italic script. His skills as an architect were so respected that in 1546 he was put in charge of the rebuilding of St. Peter's Church in Rome.

Like Leonardo da Vinci, Michelangelo helped change the direction of the Renaissance. Michelangelo's works were awe inspiring, but they were also solemn and religious. His later sculptures, particularly, conveyed a sense of human weakness, sin, sadness, and death.

Michelangelo uses marble from the quarries at Carrara, 80 miles (130 kilometers) from Florence. **Right:** *Michelangelo believes that the figure already exists within the block and that his job is simply to free it by chipping away the stone. He carves the figure out of the stone as if he is lifting it from a tank of water. His unfinished statue of a slave looks as though it is struggling to free itself from the stone that imprisons it.* **Far left:** *Michelangelo completes his statue of David for the city of Florence in 1501, when he is 26. The statue is more than 14 feet (4.25 meters) tall.* **Above left:** *Michelangelo does much to popularize the cult of the Virgin Mary in Italy. His* Pietà, *sculpted during 1498 and 1499, portrays Mary as a young woman to show the "perpetual purity of the Virgin."*

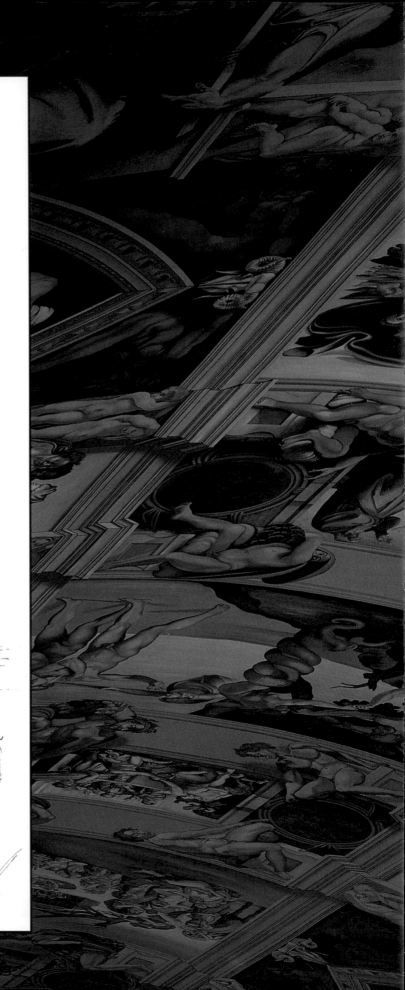

The Sistine Chapel

In 1508, Pope Julius II asked Michelangelo to paint the ceiling of the Sistine Chapel in the Vatican. Michelangelo had reservations; he claimed that he was a sculptor not a painter, but he accepted the commission. His reservations were borne out when the first scene he painted was ruined before it was finished; in his inexperience, he had used too-damp plaster and had to start over.

The huge fresco took Michelangelo four years to complete. Too ill-tempered to employ assistants, he worked mostly alone. In a poem written in 1510, he described how uncomfortable the work was:

My belly is shoved up under my chin . . .
My beard faces skyward and the back of
*   my neck is wedged into my spine . . .*
My face is richly carpeted with a thick
*   layer of paint from my brush . . .*
I don't want to be here and I'm no
*   painter.*

The relationship between the temperamental artist and the fierce pope was stormy. Julius frequently climbed up to inspect the work, and once, when Michelangelo told him he would finish "when I can," Julius threatened to throw Michelangelo from the scaffolding.

The Sistine Chapel ceiling comprises 340 figures and 5,600 square feet (520 square meters) of plaster. The biblical scenes show the story of Creation in reverse order, starting with Noah lying drunk and disgraced, and moving back to the creation of Eve, Adam, the sky and water, the sun and moon, and light.
Right: *Michelangelo's sketch shows how he had to stand to paint the frescoes.*

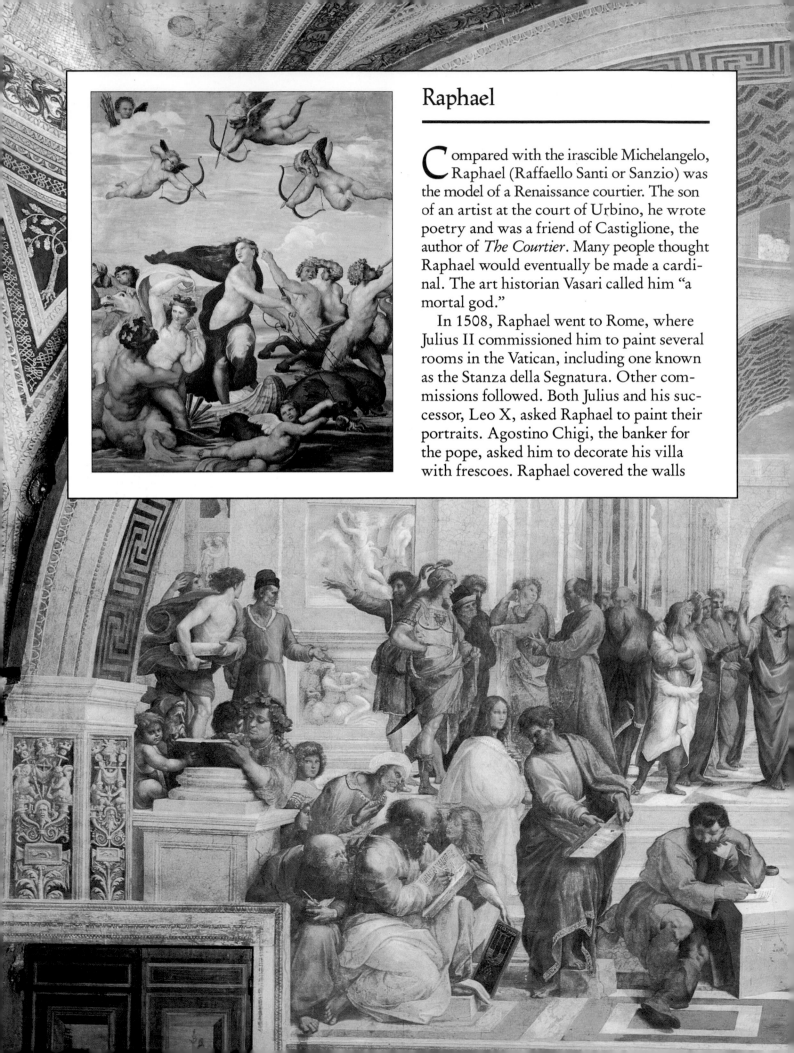

Raphael

Compared with the irascible Michelangelo, Raphael (Raffaello Santi or Sanzio) was the model of a Renaissance courtier. The son of an artist at the court of Urbino, he wrote poetry and was a friend of Castiglione, the author of *The Courtier*. Many people thought Raphael would eventually be made a cardinal. The art historian Vasari called him "a mortal god."

In 1508, Raphael went to Rome, where Julius II commissioned him to paint several rooms in the Vatican, including one known as the Stanza della Segnatura. Other commissions followed. Both Julius and his successor, Leo X, asked Raphael to paint their portraits. Agostino Chigi, the banker for the pope, asked him to decorate his villa with frescoes. Raphael covered the walls

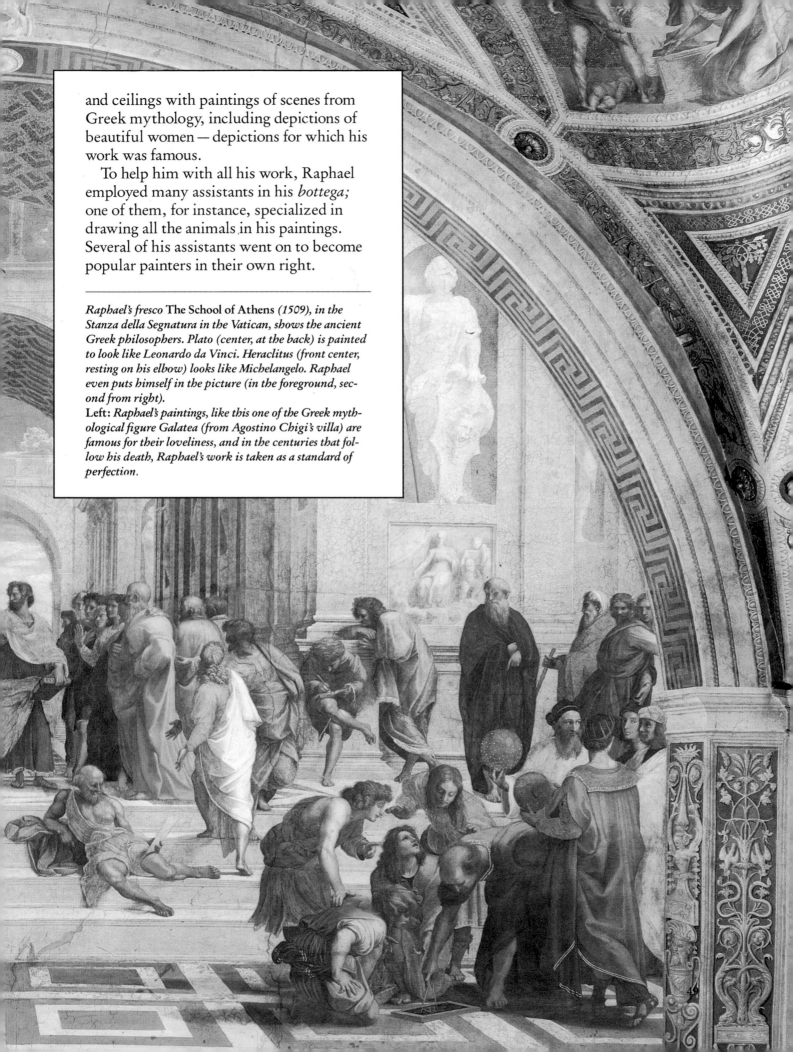

and ceilings with paintings of scenes from Greek mythology, including depictions of beautiful women — depictions for which his work was famous.

To help him with all his work, Raphael employed many assistants in his *bottega;* one of them, for instance, specialized in drawing all the animals in his paintings. Several of his assistants went on to become popular painters in their own right.

Raphael's fresco The School of Athens *(1509), in the Stanza della Segnatura in the Vatican, shows the ancient Greek philosophers. Plato (center, at the back) is painted to look like Leonardo da Vinci. Heraclitus (front center, resting on his elbow) looks like Michelangelo. Raphael even puts himself in the picture (in the foreground, second from right).*

Left: *Raphael's paintings, like this one of the Greek mythological figure Galatea (from Agostino Chigi's villa) are famous for their loveliness, and in the centuries that follow his death, Raphael's work is taken as a standard of perfection.*

Music

During the Renaissance, music was an essential part of church ceremonies and court life. It was also a common form of entertainment for ordinary people.

Renaissance writers believed that composers such as Guillaume Dufay (1400–1474) and Josquin Desprez (c. 1440–1521) had improved music as much as artists such as Donatello and Michelangelo had improved painting and sculpture. In the 1470s, Johannes de Tinctoris (c. 1435–1511), a Netherlander living in Italy, claimed that "there does not exist a single piece of music . . . worth hearing that was not composed within the last 40 years."

The musicians of the Renaissance could not imitate Greek or Roman music because it had never been written down. They could, however, read the theories of the Greek philosopher Pythagoras, who said that harmony ought to be based on mathematical intervals, especially thirds and fifths (the notes that are two and four tones above the bass note). Renaissance composers used these ideas to develop the principles of counterpoint (the art of combining voices in harmony). For the dedication of the dome of Florence's cathedral, Dufay wrote *Nuper rosarum flores*, a piece of music with harmonies based on the ratios used by Brunelleschi in his design of the dome.

Later in the Renaissance, instruments on which chords could be played, such as the lute and the harpsichord (which was invented during the Renaissance), became

popular. There was also a new respect for the meaning of the words set to musical pieces and their mood. Late-Renaissance composers often based their music on a simple tune, which was repeated in turn by the different parts.

At first, Renaissance music was dominated by Netherlanders (Josquin was the most famous). It was only toward the end of the 16th century that Italian composers such as Pierluigi da Palestrina (*c.* 1525–1594) began to make their mark.

Music notation became standardized during the Renaissance, and in 1501, in Venice, Ottaviano Petrucci printed the first music to show staves, notes, and words together. Courtiers were expected to be able to sing or play music. Isabella d'Este was an accomplished lute player, and it was at her court at Mantua that the *frottola* (a song in four parts) was developed. Composers wrote music for court dances and set the poems of Petrarch and the ancient Roman poet Virgil to music. The desire of musicians to put poetry to music led also to the development of the madrigal, a more complex composition for voices and, sometimes, instruments. During the 16th century, a group of Florentine musicians—the *Camerata fiorentina*—met to try to develop a form of music similar to that used in the classical world. This movement led, late in the century, to the development of opera.

A group of late-Renaissance musicians prepares for a performance. The two singers will be accompanied by (left to right) bass viol, lute, another bass viol, recorder, cornetto, and chitarrone (archlute).

Theater

Throughout the Middle Ages, township guilds had performed plays — known as miracle and mystery plays — on religious subjects. During the Renaissance, theater changed as writers and actors began to explore secular themes.

The first step was the discovery by humanist scholars of the Greek tragedies and comedies, which they tried to imitate. The architect Alberti wrote a comedy in Latin that was mistaken for a classical play. Other authors started to produce spectacles (for celebrations such as weddings) and court entertainments, which might involve enactments of the legends of King Arthur or famous historical events. When, as a result, the Church refused to let the actors perform any longer on the church steps, they used carts or balconies instead. In the 16th century, plays were also being written in Italian for the first time. And in 1565, the Italian architect Andrea Palladio (1508–1580) designed the first permanent theater, built of wood and modeled on ancient theaters, for a group of humanists in Vicenza. The first play performed at the theater was the Greek tragedy *Oedipus Rex*.

As the theater developed, so did the craft of acting — especially after the middle of the 16th century, when women were first allowed to perform on stage. A Renaissance actor needed a clear, loud voice and the ability to show emotion (usually this meant extreme overacting). Actors improvised their speeches and added jokes to the script to keep the audience entertained.

Venice was a center of theatrical development. Particularly famous were the playwright Angelo Beolco and the actress Vincenza Armani, a 16th-century beauty who wrote perfect Latin and composed music to accompany her own poems.

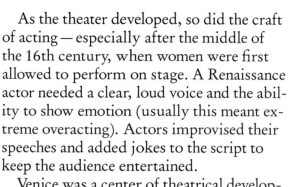

Renaissance theater is influenced by carnivals such as this festival in Siena.

Theater becomes so popular that "workers go without food to have the money to go to the play." They especially enjoy the commedia dell'arte, *a form of comic theater in which the first clowns appear. One character, Pulcinella, becomes the Punch of later Punch and Judy shows, while Harlequin (right) is a slow-witted servant who is also an excellent acrobat. If the actor playing Harlequin runs out of things to say, he hits other actors with his stick.*

Religious Upheaval

In many ways, the Renaissance, which encouraged the exploration of new ideas, was a difficult time for the Christian religion. Humanists discovered that the Vulgate Bible — a Latin translation used by the Catholic Church since the fourth century — contained mistranslations and other errors. In studying ancient authors, the humanists implied that there were other authorities on how to live life besides the Catholic Church. Scholars who read Greek texts also learned about the Greek gods. During one church service, the speaker accidentally even prayed to the "Greek immortals" (the Greek gods). Other Renaissance humanists believed that their lives were dominated by the stars, read occult writings, and practiced magic, alchemy, or witchcraft. Still, most scholars, like the Neoplatonist Ficino, believed that the teachings of classical Greek philosophers were consistent with Christianity.

There was, however, increasing dissatisfaction with the Catholic Church. Guicciardini, who had been secretary to Leo X, called the papal court "a disgrace, an example of all the shames and scandals of the world."

Eventually a disaster befell the Church. It hinged upon money. Pope Leo needed millions of ducats for his luxurious lifestyle and architectural projects (notably the rebuilding of St. Peter's Church in Rome). His methods of raising money became increasingly disreputable. In 1517, he arrested a number of cardinals who he claimed were plotting to assassinate him. He had one of them strangled, then set the rest free after they had paid fines of up to 150,000 ducats. Soon after, Leo created 31 new cardinals, requiring each of them to

pay him more than 300,000 ducats for the appointment. There was an outcry. Machiavelli thought that "the Church's ruin and punishment are at hand." The criticism was strongest in Germany, where, as Leo had been warned in 1516, thousands were waiting for a chance to speak out against the pope.

The chance came in 1517, when Leo's agent Johann Tetzel arrived in the German town of Wittenberg in Saxony. Tetzel was selling papal indulgences (pardons that promised the buyer forgiveness for any sin). "The Holy Father had the power to forgive sin and, if he forgave it, God must do so also," Tetzel preached.

This approach outraged an Augustinian monk named Martin Luther (1483–1546). On October 31, 1517, Luther nailed his Ninety-five Theses (a series of documents criticizing the sale of indulgences) to the door of the Castle Church in Wittenberg.

Luther argued that it was not good deeds that saved the believer from hell (as Tetzel claimed) but faith in Jesus Christ. In 1520, Leo issued a papal bull (act of law) declaring Luther a heretic. Nothing could be done, however, because the duke of Saxony, seeing an opportunity to free himself from the authority of the pope, protected Luther.

Other German states — Hesse, Brunswick, and Brandenburg — broke with Rome. By 1544, Denmark, England, and Sweden had also severed ties with the Church. Protestantism had been born.

Renaissance thinkers turn to authorities other than the Catholic Church to learn the meaning of life and explore the nature of the world. Alchemists, for instance, study the works of the so-called Hermes Trismegistus (written in the third century A.D.), which teach that the universe is held together by occult forces. They try to control these forces by means of spells, charms, and symbolic pictures. In this way, they hope to find the philosopher's stone, reputed to hold the secret of everlasting life and health and of power over nature.

The Sack of Rome

Though he ruled one of the most powerful states in Italy, the pope was weak compared to the two rulers who wanted to dominate Italy in the early 16th century — François I of France and Holy Roman Emperor Charles V. The pope, like many Italian rulers, was caught in the struggle between François and Charles. In 1523, Pope Clement VII (ruled 1525–1534) allied himself with François against Charles, hoping to check the threat presented by the emperor. The resulting wars raged for three years, ruining much of Italy.

In the spring of 1527, Charles assembled a large force in Milan under the command of Charles de Bourbon (1490–1527), the city's governor and an ally of the Emperor Charles. That year, François could not afford to send an army, so Clement was left to face Charles's forces alone.

Clement asked for a truce, but the emperor's troops had gone without pay for months and were eager for plunder. Rebellious, they marched south to Rome. On May 6, 1527, the soldiers broke through the walls and swarmed into the city. For eight days, they killed, raped, and looted without mercy, destroying many of the city's frescoes and statues in their frenzy. Monks and nuns were treated with particular brutality.

While Clement took refuge in the castle of Sant'Angelo, Lutherans paraded through the streets of Rome with their leader dressed as the pope, sitting on a donkey. Looters opened the tomb of St. Peter, looking for gold, and one of the German soldiers attached to his own spear the lancehead said to have pierced the side of Christ. The Vatican was used as a stable, and papal edicts and manuscripts were used as bedding for the horses.

Charles's army occupied Rome for nine months. It was said that during that time 2,000 bodies were thrown into the River Tiber, 10,000 were buried, and money and treasure worth four million ducats were looted. Eventually Charles, who was again in control of his army, agreed to release Clement for the payment of 400,000 ducats and the surrender of a number of cities. The army left in February 1528.

Although Rome recovered quite quickly from the occupation and soon regained its position as the center of the Catholic Church, the Sack of Rome was a disaster for the papacy. Since the Middle Ages, the pope had claimed that the rulers of the world owed him allegiance; the Sack showed that that claim no longer had much force. Contemporaries called the Sack a "judgment from God," and when Clement died, the people of Rome lit bonfires to celebrate, dragging his body into the streets and mutilating it.

Many historians believe the Sack of Rome marked the end of the Renaissance. Under Clement's predecessors Julius II and Leo X, Rome had stood for the promise of a universal culture uniting classical and Christian ideas. Now, all the world knew that Rome (and Italy) could not remain truly independent of the great powers of Europe. Rome could no longer consider itself the center of European civilization.

Lutheran soldiers, wearing cardinals' robes over their armor, loot and burn churches, murdering the priests.

The Renaissance Survives

Because of the Sack of Rome, many scholars and artists fled to Venice, which flourished as a center of Renaissance cultural activity in the later 16th century.

Venice was a great trading city, built on 118 small islands in a lagoon (a body of shallow water separated from the sea by sandbanks). Its merchants made their fortunes by selling the luxury goods of the East (silks and spices) to the wealthy people of the West. Every year, six fleets of trading ships were sent out — in all, 330 ships with 36,000 crewmen. They went to the Black Sea, Greece, Syria, Egypt, and north Africa, as well as to England and Flanders. The Venetian Arsenal, the dockyard where the city built its ships, was the largest industrial concern in western Europe, employing thousands of workmen. The Arsenal used assembly-line techniques and during one period of war was able to build a new ship every day for 100 days. Every vessel had standardized fittings (oars, masts, and sails, for instance), and replacement parts were kept in ports all over the known world.

According to one modern historian, the government of Venice was "the admiration and the envy of Europe." It consisted of a *doge* (duke) and a Great Council (both elected by the aristocracy of the city from among their own members), a Senate of 120 members that made laws and directed foreign affairs, and a powerful Council of Ten that administered the everyday affairs of state. The second agenda item at every Council of Ten meeting was the "denunciations," the trials of those suspected of treachery. Any citizen could denounce his or her neighbors by writing their names on a piece of paper and putting it through a hole shaped like a lion's mouth in the wall of

the *doge*'s palace.

Venice became a place of culture, scandal, and extravagance. The *doge* and the rich merchants of Venice could afford to patronize the arts. Painters such as Titian (*c.* 1490–1576) painted their portraits. The architect Palladio built villas for them all over the *terraferma* (the area of mainland Italy ruled by Venice). The writer Pietro Aretino (1492–1556) amused and shocked the wealthy Venetians with his books and plays. Also at this time, the mainland town of Padua, located in Venetian territory, had the only university medical school in Europe that insisted its students must visit the sick as part of their training.

Venice became especially famous for its music. Large numbers of professional singers and players were brought from all over Europe to perform at St. Mark's Cathedral. Musicians strove to achieve the most beautiful sounds and harmonies possible. This affected Palladio's church designs, which were the first to take into account the acoustics (effect on sound) of a building.

Although they were Catholics, the people of Venice had never fully accepted the authority of the papacy. Venetian bishops led a movement to reform the Catholic Church, and in 1536 Pope Paul III (reigned 1534–1549) asked a Venetian, Gasparo Contarini, to head a commission to look into the Church's problems. The commission marked the beginning of the process called the Counter-Reformation, which, by answering the Protestant challenge, was to save the Roman Catholic Church from collapse.

Venetian artists use bright oil paints and pay great attention to detail, as in this painting by Leandro da Ponte Bassano (1558–1623) of trade and traffic along the waterways of Venice.

The Renaissance Legacy

During the 16th century, the Italian Renaissance spread north to the rest of Europe. France and Spain attracted the best Italian talent; Leonardo da Vinci went to France to work for François I, for instance, and Titian enjoyed a long stay in the court of Charles V. The less well-known artists and scholars went to other countries. After breaking Michelangelo's nose, the sculptor Pietro Torrigiano (1472–1528) traveled to England to work in Westminster Abbey. The humanist Filippo Callimaco went to Poland, where he helped found a Polish humanist movement. The architect Aristotele Fioravanti designed St. Michael's Cathedral in the Kremlin for Czar Ivan III (ruled 1462–1505) of Russia.

At the same time, artists and scholars from all over Europe came to Italy. The German artist Albrecht Dürer (1471–1528) spent two years in Venice, from 1505 to 1507; he became fascinated with perspective and the shape of the human body, and he painted in an Italian style for most of the rest of his life. Martin Luther went to Rome in 1510 — and was horrified. Both the

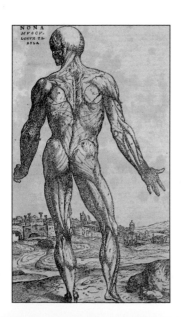

English doctor William Harvey (1578–1657), who discovered how blood circulates in the body, and the Flemish doctor Andreas Vesalius (1514–1564) studied at Padua University.

Many of the developments of the Renaissance that spread through Europe and have been handed down to our own times benefited humanity. Renaissance scholars revived the study of archaeology and history. They rejected the authority of the Church in matters of learning. In the humanities, they turned to ancient sources for ethical insight and self-knowledge, so opening the way for a tradition of independent thinking. In the domain of nature, they came to trust the results of their own observations and experiments. Their obsession with gaining knowledge of nature formed the basis for the Scientific Revolution in the 17th century and the Enlightenment of the 18th century. For this reason, many scholars see the Renaissance as the beginning of modern mathematics, science, and medicine.

This urge to explore also partly explains the important role played by Italians in the European Reconnaissance — the Renaissance exploration of the world. Christopher Columbus (1451–1506) was born in Genoa. He was a typical Renaissance man: arrogant, confident, and greedy. His studies of geography and history led him to reject the belief, supported by the Church, that the Atlantic Ocean was too wide to be crossed, and in 1492, he set sail from Spain to prove that he was right. His voyage is arguably one of the most important events in world history. In 1497, another Italian, the navigator Giovanni Caboto (known as John Cabot; 1450–1498), sailed a British ship to North America. Half a century later his son Sebastian (1476–1557) pioneered a sea route from Britain to Russia.

Less earth-shaking but still influential were the introduction of pocket-size books, the Renaissance use of italic script, and the

Renaissance development of polite manners, spread mainly through the influence of Castiglione's book *The Courtier*.

The Renaissance also sowed the seeds of disaster and suffering. The period coincided with a permanent split in western Christianity between Catholics and Protestants, which was to lead to centuries of wars, persecutions, massacres, and burnings. In politics, the Renaissance marked the beginnings of aggressive nationalism, of all-powerful rulers, and of "Machiavellian" politics — forces that threaten to destroy the world even today.

For three centuries after the Sack of Rome, Italian culture continued to dominate European thinking. Country villas were built in the classical manner. Grammar schools taught Greek and Latin. A tour of Italy was an important part of an artist's or a gentleman's education.

Nineteenth-century historians believed that the world in which they lived had been directly molded by the Renaissance. Writing in 1875, the historian J. A. Symonds commented that "Castiglione's courtier is . . . a modern gentleman, such as all men of education at the present day would wish to be." Even today, many see reflections of our own time in the Renaissance. The arrogance and self-created style of a Michelangelo, the restless curiosity of a Leonardo, even the irresponsible extravagance of a Lorenzo the Magnificent — all these may remind us of the modern individual who believes in his or her uniqueness and feels called to define a personal identity.

The Polish astronomer Nicolaus Copernicus (1473–1543) studies Greek, mathematics, and astronomy in the universities of Padua and Bologna; while in Italy, he develops the theory that the earth orbits the sun.
Left: *Andreas Vesalius's revolutionary book on anatomy,* **The Fabric of the Human Body** *(1543), is based on dissections done in Italy. It is illustrated by Jan Steven van Calcar, a German artist living in Italy, and printed in Venice.*

How Do We Know?

Historians studying the Renaissance can examine the paintings of artists such as Botticelli or Mantegna. They can marvel at the beauty of a Donatello statue or Michelangelo's majestic frescoes on the Sistine Chapel ceiling. Only a few of Leonardo da Vinci's paintings remain, but historians can study his notebooks. Brunelleschi's dome still dominates the Florence skyline, and the architecture of Palladio survives not only in the villas and palaces he built but in the hundreds of Palladian mansions that were built in imitation throughout western Europe. Because musical notation was standardized during the Renaissance, we can even play modern recordings of music composed by Palestrina.

LITERACY AND LITERATURE

Literacy (the ability to read) increased during Renaissance times, and a far greater number of written sources are available to the historian from these years than from the Middle Ages. Historians can study a vast number of manuscript sources ranging from the business accounts of Florentine merchants to the letter in which Michelangelo boasts about how he put the pope in his place. They must remember, however, that the writers might not have been telling the absolute truth.

Because printing was invented during the Renaissance, large numbers of books were published. One of Luther's books sold 4,000 copies in one month in 1520. Castiglione's book *The Courtier* was first published in Italy in 1528. The book was translated into French in 1537, Spanish in 1540, and English in 1561. In 1566, a Polish version appeared, although the translator had edited it so that it was set in Cracow instead of Urbino, and it did not have any women in it. He also omitted the sections about art and sculpture on the grounds that "we don't know about them here." Inevitably, some of the books of the Renaissance have survived — especially since many were preserved in the libraries that were set up during the period.

The Renaissance produced some great works of literature, including the poems and letters of Petrarch, the philosophy of Erasmus, the poetry of Politian, and the famous romantic epic *Orlando Furioso*, by Ariosto. Historians can read Machiavelli's plays and his bitter book on politics, *The Prince*, although they should consider that

it was written during a period of despair and failure and contradicts Machiavelli's own actions. In the same way, a historian who wants to find out about manners and personal conduct during the Renaissance might read *The Courtier,* realizing that Castiglione was writing an idealized account of the discussions at Urbino 21 years after the event and that he intended the book to be a manual on how to behave.

THE FIRST RENAISSANCE HISTORIANS

The historian of the Renaissance is also fortunate to have histories written at the time as references. Biondo and Poggio Bracciolini have been described as "the real founders of modern archaeology," and Renaissance writers revived the writing of history. Alberti, Cennini, and Vasari left us histories of Renaissance art and architecture. Leonardo Bruni and Francesco Guicciardini were not only careful historians, they also held high posts in the government and so had an inside perspective on what was really going on in the politics of the time. Historians have to be aware, however, that Renaissance writers did not try to give the objective truth but wrote so that their readers might learn the "lessons of history."

For this reason, many historians doubt some of the more extreme stories that have been handed down to us about the period. The tales of horror from the Sack of Rome, for example, may have been exaggerated by writers trying to draw a moral about the corruption of the papacy or the depravity of Lutherans; no historian has ever been able to confirm one commonly told story of a woman who killed herself during the Sack rather than be raped, or another of a father who killed his daughter to save her from the mob.

AUTHORITY AND FREEDOM OF THOUGHT

In medieval times, the laws of the government and the ideas of the Catholic Church were believed to have the authority of God. Renaissance thinkers challenged this idea. Scholars in the Renaissance came to believe that truth can be reached through reading and research, after which one must draw one's own conclusions. Of all the results of the Renaissance, this is perhaps the most important.

At the beginning of this book, we noted that some historians think of the Renaissance as the beginning of the modern age. You should now be able to decide for yourself if this is true. Remember, though, that the very idea of discovering the answer to a question by reading a book and then making up your own mind was in part a Renaissance invention.

Above left: *Paintings provide information about life in Renaissance times; for instance, this detail from* **The Mass at Bolsena** *by Raphael shows several members of the Swiss Guard, who protected the pope. Their uniforms were designed by Leonardo da Vinci.*
Below left: *In this diagram, the 16th-century French humanist Charles de Bouelles (c. 1479–1553) suggests that there are four levels of humanity: A lazy person merely exists (in Latin,* est) *like a stone. A greedy person might be said to live (*vivit*) like a plant, and a vain person to feel (*sentit*) like an animal. Only the scholar who thinks (*intelligit*), however, is fully human.*
Below: *An astronomical chart (c. 1543) based on Copernicus's theories.*

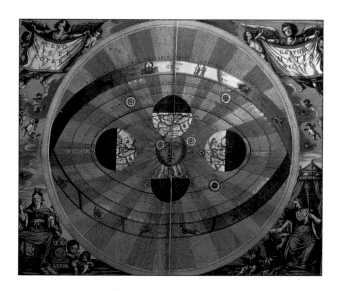

Index

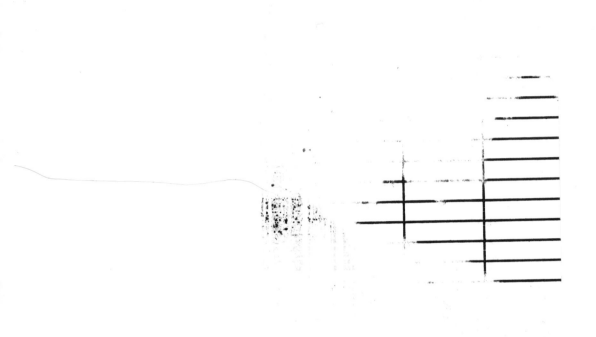

Important
Events

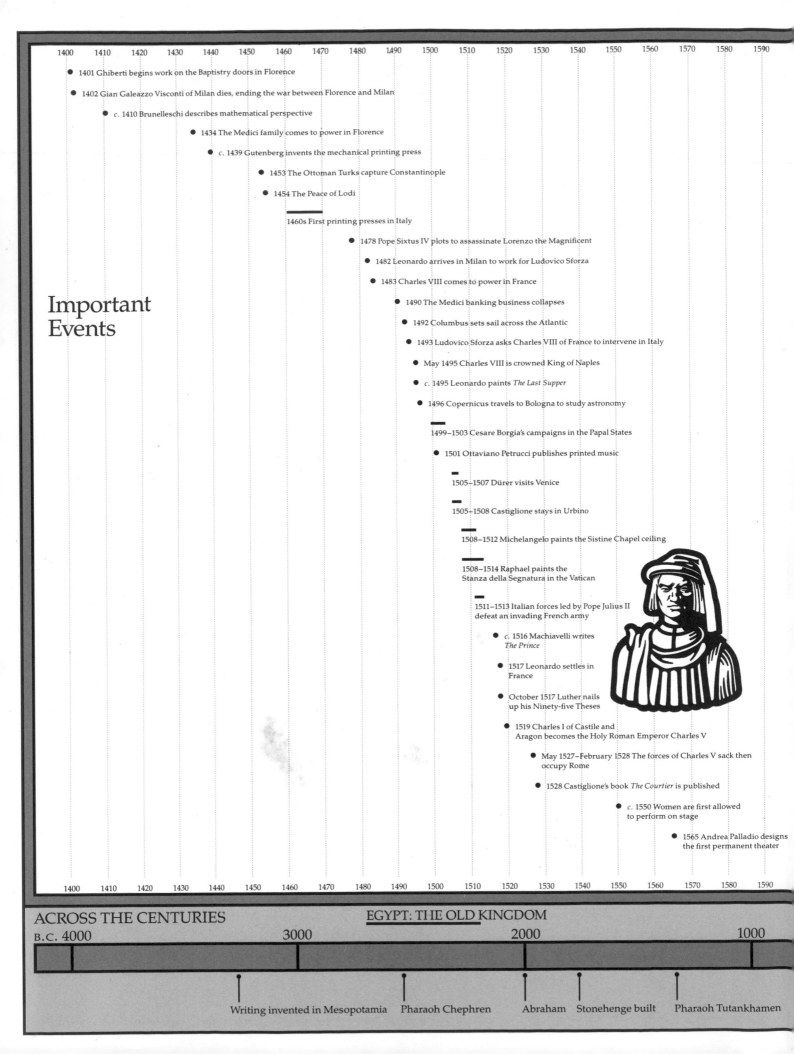

| 1400 | 1410 | 1420 | 1430 | 1440 | 1450 | 1460 | 1470 | 1480 | 1490 | 1500 | 1510 | 1520 | 1530 | 1540 | 1550 | 1560 | 1570 | 1580 | 1590 |

- 1401 Ghiberti begins work on the Baptistry doors in Florence
- 1402 Gian Galeazzo Visconti of Milan dies, ending the war between Florence and Milan
- c. 1410 Brunelleschi describes mathematical perspective
- 1434 The Medici family comes to power in Florence
- c. 1439 Gutenberg invents the mechanical printing press
- 1453 The Ottoman Turks capture Constantinople
- 1454 The Peace of Lodi

1460s First printing presses in Italy

- 1478 Pope Sixtus IV plots to assassinate Lorenzo the Magnificent
- 1482 Leonardo arrives in Milan to work for Ludovico Sforza
- 1483 Charles VIII comes to power in France
- 1490 The Medici banking business collapses
- 1492 Columbus sets sail across the Atlantic
- 1493 Ludovico Sforza asks Charles VIII of France to intervene in Italy
- May 1495 Charles VIII is crowned King of Naples
- c. 1495 Leonardo paints *The Last Supper*
- 1496 Copernicus travels to Bologna to study astronomy

1499–1503 Cesare Borgia's campaigns in the Papal States

- 1501 Ottaviano Petrucci publishes printed music

1505–1507 Dürer visits Venice

1505–1508 Castiglione stays in Urbino

1508–1512 Michelangelo paints the Sistine Chapel ceiling

1508–1514 Raphael paints the
Stanza della Segnatura in the Vatican

1511–1513 Italian forces led by Pope Julius II
defeat an invading French army

- c. 1516 Machiavelli writes
  The Prince
- 1517 Leonardo settles in
  France
- October 1517 Luther nails
  up his Ninety-five Theses
- 1519 Charles I of Castile and
  Aragon becomes the Holy Roman Emperor Charles V
- May 1527–February 1528 The forces of Charles V sack then
  occupy Rome
- 1528 Castiglione's book *The Courtier* is published
- c. 1550 Women are first allowed
  to perform on stage
- 1565 Andrea Palladio designs
  the first permanent theater

| 1400 | 1410 | 1420 | 1430 | 1440 | 1450 | 1460 | 1470 | 1480 | 1490 | 1500 | 1510 | 1520 | 1530 | 1540 | 1550 | 1560 | 1570 | 1580 | 1590 |

ACROSS THE CENTURIES   EGYPT: THE OLD KINGDOM

B.C. 4000   3000   2000   1000

Writing invented in Mesopotamia   Pharaoh Chephren   Abraham   Stonehenge built   Pharaoh Tutankhamen